Learning to Minister Under the Anointing

Healing Ministry in Your Church

RANDY CLARK

Global Awakening
1451 Clark Street
Mechanicsburg, PA 17055

1-866-AWAKENING

www.globalawakening.com

Global Awakening
{ Core Message Series }

It is our desire to bring the messages of the Kingdom to the people of God. We have taken what we consider to be core messages from Randy Clark's sermons and schools and printed some of them in booklet form. We hope this teaching increases your understanding of God's purposes for the times we are in and that you find yourself encouraged in your faith. Other core messages are available and they are listed at the end of this booklet.

Table of Contents

Acknowledgements

The suggestions discussed in this booklet are drawn from my experience and the experience of many different local church pastors I have met through my work. I want to express my appreciation in particular to Pastors Bill Johnson and Tom Jones, and to Tom Ruotolo, for their considerable contributions.

My warmest thanks and remembrance for the late John Mackenzie, a longtime Global Awakening Associate, former board member and dear friend,who put into written form (in the original edition) this message which on my heart for the church of today.

My hope is that this booklet will be the beginning, if it has not already begun, of an exciting adventure for **you** and **your church**, where you will see the power of the Holy Spirit moving through your people as they pray for the sick and reach out to the lost.

May God bless you richly!

Randy Clark
Mechanicsburg, PA

Learning to Minister Under the Anointing

Preface

It has been a number of years since I wrote the original edition of this booklet. Much of it came from my experience in being used of God in what is known as the "The Toronto Blessing." The intervening years have continued to validate the relevance of this little volume's subject matter. We have now taken thousands of people with us around the world, training them to minister under the anointing of the Holy Spirit. These "little ole' mes" have seen healings, miracles, and deliverances happen as they followed the simple truths and practical suggestions presented here while operating under the Holy Spirit's leading and guidance.

Two things should be noted about this edition:

1. It is still a brief introduction to the topic. It outlines very basic information, providing a useful, easily digested guide. More in-depth material is available in our other publications, including our Ministry Team Training Manual and in the manuals we use to accompany our Schools of Healing and Impartation, which we hold in various locations around the U. S. and the world.[1]

2. The material is essentially unchanged, but has been restructured and revised for clarity—including updated time references, along with some minor expansion of the material.

I hope that these modest changes improve its usefulness.

Randy Clark, April 2007

---

[1] *Please see the copyright page for contact information to obtain these and other instructional materials*

Introduction

Have you ever tried learning how to dance with a new partner? I don't know too much about dancing, but I do know that someone has to lead and the other person has to follow. There cannot be two leaders nor two followers. It is essential that one leads while the other follows. There is no negotiation on this point.

Learning to minister in the Spirit is like learning to dance. We must remember that Jesus is the leader and that we, as the Bride of Christ, must learn how to follow His lead. That is the real secret to ministering under the anointing of the Holy Spirit. Much like slow dancing, the closer you are held, the easier it is to sense the movement of the Leader— increasing your ability to follow His direction. We need to learn how to relax, rest in the Holy Spirit's presence, and follow His lead. Like learning to dance, it takes time and practice to learn to minister in cooperation with the Holy Spirit. There is a process that we must all go through as He teaches us. There are things that we will do right and there are other things we will do wrong, but the important thing is for us to press on and grow in our experience so that we may increasingly be a vessel of blessing.

This booklet was not written as a theological framework for you to believe in the things that I'm writing about or to try to convince you that the things described within these pages are real and are of God–I am assuming that that has already been established in your mind and heart, and that you are ready to jump in and learn to minister under the Holy Spirit's guidance. Though we talk a lot about flowing with the Holy Spirit, we don't, when it comes down to it, know how to cooperate with God, or the practical ways to recognize when one is flowing in that anointing. This booklet is intended to be a practical guide to help you, the reader, in these things.

I've been ministering for many years now and I hope that what I have learned may aid you in learning to minister under the anointing of God. There are many different ways to minister in co-operation with the Spirit of God. In sharing my experiences and insights into my understanding of this way of ministering, I do not want to give the impression that my insights are the only way to minister in the Spirit.

The central focus, in my mind, is that it is all about having relationship with the Holy Spirit. The more time we spend in the presence of God and building a relationship with Him, the more we will become sensitive to Him and His ways (Exodus 33:13). Relationship is only built as we daily spend time with Him. We must, first and foremost, learn to follow His lead as we press into Him everyday. In the prayer ministry guidelines that follow, that is our underlying theme.

Prayer Ministry Guidelines

"If you remain in me and my words remain in you, ask whatever you wish, and it will be given you" (John 15:7).

The goal of prayer is the release of God's restorative and redemptive love, life, and power in the lives of those to whom we minister. When we look at the ministry of Jesus, we see that, anointed by the Holy Spirit and power, He "went around doing good and healing all who were under the power of the devil, because God was with him" (Acts 10:38). Under the anointing of the Person of the Holy Spirit, we too can follow the example of our Lord Jesus.

The early days of the Toronto outpouring were a great time during which I learned many practical insights about how to minister under the anointing of God. These came primarily through observation while praying for literally thousands of people during the first few weeks of those meetings. I began to teach the insights that I was learning to the ministry teams that I was training — in my own church as well as in other churches. I hope the following review of those insights is helpful to you. Some of the things I touch on in this "guidelines" chapter I will cover in more depth later. In this chapter I want to give you a "big picture" view. Let's get started.

Pray with your eyes open

I began to teach those on ministry teams to pray with their eyes open so that they could see what the Father was doing. In my opinion, this is one of the reasons that Jesus was so effective in His ministry—He learned how to cooperate with the Father in what He was doing. Jesus only did what He saw the Father do, and He only said what He heard the Father say. Jesus said of Himself:

> *"I tell you the truth, the Son can do nothing by himself; he can do only what he sees his Father doing, because whatever the Father does the Son also does." (John 5:19).*

Jesus—under the anointing and power of the Holy Spirit— only did what He saw the Father doing. This is also essential for a maturing effectiveness in prayer ministry.

How to "See" What the Father is Doing

What does it mean—practically speaking—to "see" what the Father is doing? When we speak of seeing the Holy Spirit on an individual, we do not mean that we actually see a visible form of the Holy Spirit on that person, although that may happen in some instances. He may give other direction through various biblical forms of revelation. Most often, what we have learned to recognize are the effects of the presence and activity of the Holy Spirit upon the human body. For example, often when the Holy Spirit begins to touch someone, their autonomic nervous system is affected: their eye lids may begin to flutter, their breathing may change—getting either slower or faster, their body may begin to heat up, causing them to perspire, and their fingers and hands will often begin to tremble.

One particular phenomenon I often see is what I call the "Blessing of Peace" (I will cover more on this in a later chapter). When this happens, a look of peace and rest comes upon a person—often seen in their facial expressions and body language. Many times the person's shoulders will sag slightly from the affects of what is felt. When I see that peace being manifested, I will usually say, "There it is. Take it." Sometimes, if you do not encourage them in this way, the person will try to control what is happening and stop themselves from falling,[2] causing ministry to that person to be hindered or take much longer.

Let me say at this point that I do not believe that you have to fall in the Spirit to receive from God. However, many people receive a lot when they do rest in the Spirit. I encourage people not to force themselves to stand and resist the Holy Spirit, and I also encourage them not to make themselves fall and help the Holy Spirit. Both of these responses are of the flesh. We want people to relax and receive all that God has for them in the way that He wants to touch them. Many may fall and others may not fall—as each receives from God in various ways.

Receive All That the Father Has for That Moment

I instruct the ones that are receiving ministry to remain on the floor if they fall until it is no longer difficult for them to move or to get up. I explain that they will know it is time to get off the floor when it takes no more will power than normal to move and to get up. If it is difficult to move, then they should not try to, because God is still working. They should enjoy the peace of God as long they still feel its manifest presence. I found that too many people get up too quickly. Many times people try to get up before God is done touching them and they miss out on so much God still wants to do and impart.

---

2 *The assumption here is that—for efficiency of space and time— people are lined up in rows next to one another waiting for prayer ministry. We discuss "catching" to prevent injury and facilitate ministry in a later chapter.*

Thank God for What He is Doing

When you see the Spirit begin to touch someone, thank the Lord for what He is doing. This is most effective when you thank Him out loud, so that the person receiving ministry can hear you. I do this out loud for two reasons. First, this reverences and honors the person and ministry of the Holy Spirit. Secondly, it reassures the person being prayed for that what they are beginning to experience is from the Holy Spirit. When they hear you thanking God for what He is doing, then they are reassured that it is not something that they are initiating or imagining.

For example, if the physical signs indicate a "Blessing of Peace" is occurring, then bless what God is doing. One of the ways of expressing thanks is to acknowlede out loud what you see the Father doing. You can do this by saying, "I bless Your peace. Thank you, Holy Spirit. More peace."

Don't "Get Stuck," Keep Moving

Another very important way that I learned to minister under the anointing of God was to not stay too long with someone when ministering to them. If someone does not begin to receive within a reasonable amount of time, I will usually move on to the next person and come back to that person later or have someone else stay and "soak" them in prayer. Staying too long with a person can sometimes drain your own faith and anointing as well as create an atmosphere of doubt rather than faith in the entire congregation. Many times, moving on to someone else who more quickly receives encourages the one having difficulty receiving as they see the Holy Spirit ministering to the other. Of course don't make this a rule or law. There are occasions where the Holy Spirit will move very powerfully on one person as a catalyst for faith and the release of miracles. In this case, don't move on prematurely, but be sensitive to bless all that He wants to accomplish in that moment.

Since some people need more time than others to receive, it is great if you can have an apprentice/assistant with you who can stay behind with someone who is receiving and needs a little more time to soak in the presence of God. I tell my assistant to stay a few minutes longer and soak the person in prayer, then catch up to me.

Adapt Prayer Team Ministry to Crowd Size

The amount of time that you spend with each person depends on the size of the ministry team and the size of the crowd. If you have many people receiving ministry and not too many ministering, then it is best to spend less time with each person. When you have a larger ministry team with fewer people, then you can obviously spend more time with each individual. Praying for two people at once can be very helpful at times as well. To do this, just place each hand on a different person in the prayer line.

If you find yourself with a lot of people to minister to and do not have enough people on the ministry team to help, I often recommend lining the people up in lines to pray for them. I have sometimes asked the pastors of the churches to put down masking tape every eight feet on the floor where we will be ministering. I tell them that I am going to go through the line quickly, praying for each person very briefly—that there will be some who will receive quickly, and others who will need more time to receive. I then come back around and pray again very briefly for those who didn't seem to receive as much as the others the first time. I will repeat this continually assuring them that it is okay to take longer as we are all different. This process allows those who are what I term "easy-to-receive" to get ministry and after some time to get up and yield their floor space to others who have been waiting for a turn to receive prayer.

Help those who don't easily receive

Something I have noticed is that when I begin to pray for someone, if their eyebrow wrinkles up, it is usually very difficult for them to receive. This usually indicates that their body is beginning to get tense. It is much easier to receive from God when you are in a relaxed posture than if you are in an apprehensive one. If you have the time and can dialogue with them, often the issue will be revealed and can be prayed through, after which they can receive much more easily. Let us now look a little more in-depth at this issue of receiving.

Receiving

"And with that he breathed on them and said, 'Receive the Holy Spirit'"(John 20:22).

The Holy Spirit is a Person

In learning to minister under the anointing, it is essential to remember that the Holy Spirit is the Person of the Godhead with whom, to use our previous illustration, we are dancing. He is the Leader. He is the source of life, gifting, and power, yes, but all ministry flows from relationship with this exceedingly kind, gracious, caring Person, who is NOT just a force. When you receive the Person of the Holy Spirit, you are receiving everything that He is. Too often we intellectualize what it means to "receive the Holy Spirit" into one or more "events." Father desires that it be an ever increasing reception of the One that desires to dwell within (see John 14:16-17, 25).

There are two common ways in which I have seen the Person of the Holy Spirit come to us. For the sake of communication, I call them "The Blessing of Peace" and "The Blessing of Power."

The Blessing of Peace

"And the peace of God, which transcends all understanding, will guard your hearts and your minds in Christ Jesus" (Philippians 4:7) .

One of the first things I learned during the first few weeks of the meetings at the Toronto Airport Vineyard (now Toronto Airport Christian Fellowship) was the value of what I call the "Blessing of Peace." This was an important blessing to me because only a few months before I had been on the verge of an emotional breakdown. I came under the anointing of God and fell to the floor where I rested in this deep peace that was unlike anything that I had ever experienced before. After I got up off of the floor, I had been totally set free by this peace, the peace of God transcended my understanding, touched my heart and brought peace to my mind in a way I had not previously known.

As I was ministering in Toronto during the early days of that move of God, I became deeply aware of the importance of this "Blessing of Peace." Many people fell to the floor night after night under the anointing of the Holy Spirit and experienced this "Blessing of Peace" as I prayed for them. There were literally thousands of people who were having the same kind of experiences, where the peace of God would touch them in ways they had previously never experienced. Many of those not only received peace, but were healed of deep psychological wounds as well, as they rested in His Presence there on the floor.

My first awareness that I needed to teach people about the value of this blessing was when a very upset Vineyard pastor came to me. He said, "I'm frustrated. I come all this way, and I am not getting anything." I decided to ask him what had happened to him and his response was, "I was prayed for and fell to the floor, but nothing happened."

I said, "Tell me again what happened. You said you were prayed for, fell on the floor, but nothing happened?" We went through this several times. Then I said, "Your problem is that you are bringing to this new experience the paradigm from your former experiences in the Vineyard, which is equating power with shaking and feeling electricity." I explained to him that this blessing was different than what he was used to experiencing. I showed him that often when people fell, God was blessing them and filling them with His peace–not just His manifest power. I encouraged him to return to the area of ministry and receive prayer again. I told him that if he fell this time, he should not jump up right away, but should remain there on the floor and give God an opportunity to touch him in a different way. The pastor did this and discovered a wonderful new experience with the Lord— that of deep and abiding peace.

I believe that there is also a valuable lesson to be learned from my experience with this Vineyard Pastor. Many times God shows up in ways we do not expect or that we are not used to. We may be so used to Him coming in great power and shaking people that when He comes in peace we don't recognize Him because we are looking for the great power. We are to be full of expectation for God, but we must not limit Him to our own thinking of how He is supposed to come. We are to expect God Himself—not just one or two ways that God comes.

The Blessing of Power

"But you will receive power when the Holy Spirit comes on you; and you will be my witnesses..." (Acts 1:8) .

I would like to speak about the manifest power of the Lord that I've seen come upon many people as they received prayer. When you receive the Person of the Holy Spirit, you receive power. Jesus told his disciples to wait in Jerusalem until they were "clothed with power from on high" (Luke 24:49). This empowerment was for them to be effective witnesses in life and ministry. When asked by His disciples when He was going to set up His political reign, Jesus replied, "It is not for you to know the times or dates the Father has set by his own authority. But you will receive power when the Holy Spirit comes on you; and you will be my witnesses..." (Acts 1:7-8). Many times while praying for people, you will see God pour out His Spirit on people to empower them for ministry. This is often seen with visible signs of electricity or power being manifested in the person's body. Again there are no laws, many feel nothing and go home with explosive power released later as they minister.

I've watched visible demonstrations of God's power manifested in people's bodies as I laid hands on them and prayed for them. Many times I have observed people beginning to shake— sometimes quite violently. Sometimes those receiving prayer fall to the ground, where they continue to shake, while at other times they just stand upright and bounce up and down. Often this shaking is caused by a sensation of high voltage electricity surging through their body. When I see these physical phenomena, I thank God for the power with which He is enduing His people. I bless what I see the Father doing, and continue to watch and stand in amazement at what God does.

When it comes to the Blessing of Power, many times there are waves of the Holy Spirit. If you've ever been to the ocean, you can see how the waves come in and go out. They keep coming with slight intervals in between—wave after wave. When the power of God comes in these waves, it is almost as if God gives the person being touched brief respites. I say this because often the anointing is so powerful that it is physically painful. There have been some that have experienced pain in their muscles and joints for days afterward at the intensity of the anointing.

I like to instruct the person receiving ministry that there are often waves of the Spirit and to stay focused on God, waiting for all the waves to come. Many often get up too fast after only one or two waves of God's Spirit are poured out on them. God has so much more to pour out on us if we will only learn to wait on Him and receive from Him. I will usually say to the Holy Spirit, "We don't want to miss anything you want to do. We are waiting here in order to give place for You to come again and touch this person." We can't do anything unless He comes and touches— when He is done, so are we.

Don't Limit or Categorize What the Holy Spirit is Doing

I do not want to limit or categorize falling, shaking, laughing or any other type of movement to mean a specific thing. It would be foolish to try to limit God in such a manner as that. Oftentimes He comes in ways that we do not expect. I did begin to notice that there were some things which occurred often enough to describe as common patterns in how many people respond to the Holy Spirit, such as I have described above concerning the "Blessing of Peace" and "Blessing of Power."

Responding to Waves of Power

When it came to healing, we often had to tell the people after the first wave of power had come upon them to stay focused, because often God came in waves with pauses between them to allow the person receiving prayer a break from the intensity of His Presence. Helping them stay focused or in an attitude of receptivity is important. Many people are used to receiving quick prayers of pronouncements, which they are "to believe" or "stand for" and are not used to waiting upon the Holy Spirit to actually manifest the healing they have asked for.

"Dialing Down" Fleshly Control and Responses

Often in the meetings I instruct people with the following, "We do not want any courtesy drops tonight. That would be the flesh. However, if you try to stand, that is the flesh also. Don't try to fall. Don't try to stand up. Both are flesh."

One of the problems many people have is that of analysis. Borrowing from John Arnott, I would instruct people to:

> "...get out of analysis and into romance. Experiencing God is a thing of romance, not analysis. Analysis ruins it. For example did you know that the human mouth has more germs in it than any other part of the human body? Why would two adults put their mouths together with all those germs? Because they are focused not on analysis, but rather, they're caught up in romance. What you need to do is quiet your spirit and pucker up."

Humor often helps lift the pressure people put on themselves.

One of the most difficult things to do is to get people to stop praying when they are being prayed for. This is especially true for those who have been in the church longer, and for certain types of people who feel it is important to pray in tongues when receiving or to say something like, "I believe, I believe, I receive, and I receive." I have observed that it is much more difficult for people to receive when they are praying and claiming instead of resting and receiving.

.

Ministering Deliverance

"Heal the sick, raise the dead, cleanse those who have leprosy, drive out demons. Freely you have received, freely give" (Matthew 10:8).

The Need for Deliverance Ministry

When I first went to the Toronto Airport Vineyard, I noticed how often they ministered to people who were demonized. During the first week there, I told others from my staff that either the Airport Vineyard was out of balance regarding ministry to the demonized, or the St. Louis Vineyard (where I pastored at the time) was out of balance. When I finally left Toronto for an extended time, I asked John and Carol Arnott to come to my church to train my leaders in ministering to those that were demonized. Later, Carol Arnott came with a team to teach the "Healing of Past Hurts" seminar, and Paul White (who in my opinion was the most gifted Vineyard pastor ministering to the demonized in Ontario) and an associate came and led a more in-depth seminar on healing the demonized. I realized my church had been the one out of balance regarding ministry to the demonized.

Deliverance—called by some the ministry of liberation—is setting a person free from the oppression of demonic power. Many in the world, and in the church for that matter, are oppressed in some area of their life by a demonic spirit. I learned that the word "demon-possessed" in the Bible was not the best translation of what the Greek was actually describing. I prefer to use the term "demonized" or "oppression" instead, because "possession" implies that the demon has ownership and complete control over all of a person's life. However, the demoniac in Mark 5 wasn't so "possessed" that he couldn't worship Jesus. He still had enough control over his own body that he could run to Jesus and fall at His feet so that Jesus could bring Him freedom.

I learned that deliverance was central to the ministry of Jesus. It was just as central to His ministry as preaching, teaching and healing the sick (Mt. 10:7-8; Mk 16:15-17). When Mark tells the story of Jesus in his gospel, deliverance is mentioned often as one of Jesus' "other works."

> *That evening after the sunset the people brought to Jesus all the sick and demon-possessed. The whole town gathered at the door, and Jesus healed many who had various diseases. He also drove out many demons, but he would not let the demons speak because they knew who he was (Mark 1:32-34).*

Later, Mark writes about Jesus,
> *So he traveled throughout Galilee, preaching in their synagogues and driving out demons (Mark 1:39).*

Not only was deliverance central to the ministry of Jesus, but in the Great Commission He commands His disciples to make it central to their ministry as well.

> *He said to them, "Go into all the world and preach the good news to all creation. Whoever believes*

> *and is baptized will be saved, but whoever does not believe will be condemned. And these signs will accompany those who believe: In my name they will drive out demons...they will place their hands on sick people, and they will get well"* (Mark 16:15-17a; 19b).

Now for every believer, the Gospel consists of teaching/preaching, healing the sick, and casting out demons. Since this ministry was central to the ministry of Jesus and central to the early disciples, then it must be a central ministry of ours as well. God calls us to take up this ministry of deliverance to the demonized.

The Ten-step Deliverance Model

We must have a loving approach to deliverance so that we don't hurt the individual or cause embarrassment. I found a model that I like to use in different ministry settings when demons begin to manifest. It is a very efficient, loving, ten-step model for ministering deliverance from Pablo Bottari. For many years, he ran the deliverance tents for Carlos Annocondia during the Argentine revival. I want to briefly give to you these steps:[3]

1) Give the individual priority.

When ministering to someone that is demonized, we need to keep a loving attitude with the individual. We are to be firm in breaking the demon's power. Again, we are ministering to the person and they need to feel loved and accepted by the one doing ministry. I don't know too many people that would feel loved and accepted if we were yelling in their face for the demon to leave. Many of us mistake the level of our voice with the authority that Jesus gives us.

---

[3] *If you want to find out more information about the 10-step model, you can study our "Ministry Team Training Manual" or listen to a CD series, "Deliverance", by Pablo Bottari. Both are available through our bookstore: www.globalawakening. com/store*

It is our job to be encouraging with the individual and raise hope in them. It is crucial that we emphasize the overcoming power of Jesus to bring victory, drawing their attention away from the power of the demon (see 1 John 3:8b, 2 Corinthians 2:4).

2) If a spirit is manifesting, or if one manifests during your ministry, make the spirit be quiet and submit to you in the Name of Jesus.

Here is where you take authority over the spirit and command it to submit in the name of Jesus. This may take some time, but be persistent until the demon submits. Remember that you have the authority over it and it must obey you. This is vital because it leads us to the third step.

3) Establish and maintain communication with the person receiving prayer.

This is the place where you begin to talk to the person receiving prayer. Find out their name and see how they are doing. We don't want to establish communication with the demon. We want to converse with the person that is demonized.

The demon may manifest while you are trying to talk to the person. Just command the demon to submit and continue to talk to the person receiving prayer. Calling the person by name is an excellent way to keep communication after the demon tries to manifest again.

4) Ask the person receiving prayer what they want to be free from and try to make sure they actually want to get free.

Most likely there will be a habit that the person is unsuccessfully trying to break or some conduct that he or she considers odd or unfamiliar. The person must want to be free before you lead them in deliverance.

If a person doesn't want to be free and they get delivered, then the demon will end up coming back. Jesus said that when this happens the demon goes and gets seven other spirits that are more wicked than itself, and they go and live in that place from which it came (Matthew 12:43-45). Unless God sovereignly intervenes, then the person will not get and stay free if they don't want to. They must renounce and repent of anything they have been involved in that opened the door to the demonization.

5) Make sure the person receiving prayer has accepted Jesus as his Savior and Lord.

The demonized person needs the help of the Holy Spirit if they want to stay free. If they are not a Christian, then they will probably be back in bondage soon after being delivered. If this is the case, perhaps you can lead them to Christ. If they don't want to accept Jesus as their Lord and Savior then you want to pray for them and bless them, but you don't want to do deliverance on them. Again, don't turn this into law. I prayed for a man in India that suffered from headaches caused by a spirit of affliction. His deliverance from them led to his giving his life over to the Lordship of Jesus. Sometimes they want to accept Christ but are not able because of the spirit's resistance. In that case, you want to proceed with deliverance so that they are unbound and able to receive Christ.

6) Interview the person receiving ministry to discover the event(s), relationship(s), or situation(s) which have led to the bondage(s).

In this interview process, you want to look for the "open doors" that gave the spirit access into the person's life. Traumatic experiences and the person's relationship with his or her parents are good places to begin.

As I write in our "Ministry Team Training Manual", "The purpose of the interview is to expose the places where forgiveness is required, where healing is needed, and where repentance and breaking of bondages is needed. These places are open doors."

This will probably take you the longest in the whole deliverance session. This is where you want to get as much information as possible to see where these "open doors" are. Be sure to be patient and loving. Key is listening to the Holy Spirit as you are interviewing the person. He will make the whole process a lot easier if you listen to Him as you go through this. Remember, He leads; you follow in the "dance" of ministry under the anointing.

7) Lead the person receiving prayer in "closing" these doors to the admission of spirits.

When you lead this person in closing the doors, you will want them to repeat a prayer that you pray. You want to make sure that they:

- Forgive the one who has caused hurt or led him into the wrong conduct.

- Specifically repent for each sin committed in the situation and ask God's forgiveness of each.

- Renounce in the Name of Jesus all the spirits involved.

- Break the bondage caused by the sin, the conduct, the attitude, the spirit, the vow, or the curse in the Name of the Lord Jesus.

You want to make sure to go through all of these very specifically, so that all "open doors" can be closed and the spirits' access to the individual will be cut off completely.

8) Cast out the unclean spirit(s) in the name of Jesus.

This is where you command the spirits to go in the name of Jesus. You don't have to send them somewhere – you simply cast them out. Sometimes people will manifest in different ways as this step is taking place. Many people just feel lighter after this step takes place with no other manifestation than that.

NOTE: You may have to repeat steps 6, 7, and 8 multiple times before you can go on to 9 and 10. Don't be discouraged by this – you want to be very thorough with the person so that all the "open doors" are closed. Again, be led of the Spirit. Sometimes God will work on things in steps. Don't go further beyond the Holy Spirit.

9) Join the person receiving prayer in praise and thanks to the Lord Jesus for the deliverance.

If the person receiving prayer cannot thank Jesus or there is a demonic manifestation that takes place, then that is a sign that more doors need to be closed and more spirits need to go in the Name of Jesus. Otherwise, thank the Lord out loud for what He has done.

10) Ask the person to pray for the Holy Spirit's infilling and to fill all the places formerly occupied by the evil spirits.

Spend some time in prayer asking the Holy Spirit to fill the individual and letting the person that was demonized to ask the Holy Spirit to fill him. This is one of the most important steps in this process. You want to make sure that all the places that were occupied by the enemy are now filled by the Holy Spirit.

Dependence on the Holy Spirit in Deliverance

Again, this is about a relationship with the Holy Spirit. These ten steps are a model for deliverance. All models are only an invitation to experience something greater in the realms of the Spirit. This model of deliverance is an entry point to hear the Holy Spirit and cooperate with Him. Don't sacrifice the relationship and cooperation with the Holy Spirit for the model. You may need to adjust this model to bring deliverance to the person to whom you are ministering. The key is intimacy with the Holy Spirit— it is only in Him that you find what you need to bring freedom to those who are bound.

A Final Word of Caution

Let me give a word of caution here: We are not to become demon focused. As we focus on the Lord, He will show us where deliverance is needed. Seldom did this ministry occur during the meetings I led. We did not want the focus of the meetings to shift from the joy, peace, and empowering presence of God that was happening over to the demonic. When deliverances did occur in the ministry areas, we removed the person from the meetings to minister to them, so it did not distract from what God was doing cooperately.[4]

---

[4] To learn more about deliverance, I would also highly recommend a book called "Unbound: A Practical Guide to Deliverance" written by Neal Lozano or "Deliverance from Evil Spirits" by Francis MacNutt. Both are available through our website.

Ministering Healing

"Stretch out your hand to heal and perform miraculous signs and wonders through the name of your holy servant Jesus" (Acts 4:30).

I am deeply indebted to John Wimber and Blaine Cook, who have influenced me more than anyone else in the area of healing. The five-step prayer model that they taught helped me tremendously. I want to share about this prayer model in the healing section because of how it relates to praying for the sick. It has a biblical foundation in the accounts of the blind man who was healed in John 9, and in the boy who was demonized whom Jesus healed after coming down from the Mount of Transfiguration in Mark 9:14-29. Jesus interviewed the boy's father and the blind man while He was ministering to them.

Let us look at the demonized boy in Mark chapter 9:

When they [Jesus, Peter, James and John] came [from the Mount of Transfiguration] to the other disciples, they saw a large crowd around them and the teachers of the law arguing with them. As soon as all the people saw Jesus, they were

*overwhelmed with wonder and ran to greet him.
"What are you arguing with them about?" he
asked.*

*A man in the crowd answered, "Teacher, I
brought you my son, who is possessed by a spirit
that has robbed him of speech. Whenever it seizes
him, it throws him to the ground. He foams at
the mouth, gnashes his teeth and becomes rigid.
I asked your disciples to drive out the spirit, but
they could not."*

*"O unbelieving generation," Jesus replied, "how
long shall I stay with you? How long shall I put
up with you? Bring the boy to me."*

*So they brought him. When the spirit saw Jesus,
it immediately threw the boy into a convulsion.
He fell to the ground and rolled around, foaming
at the mouth.*

*Jesus asked the boy's father, "How long has he
been like this?"*

*"From childhood," he answered. "It has often
thrown him into fire or water to kill him. But if
you can do anything, take pity on us and help
us."*

*"'If you can'?" said Jesus. "Everything is possible
for him who believes."*

*Immediately the boy's father exclaimed, "I do
believe; help me overcome my unbelief!"*

*When Jesus saw that a crowd was running to the
scene, he rebuked the evil spirit. "You deaf and
mute spirit," he said, "I command you, come out*

of him and never enter him again."
The spirit shrieked, convulsed him violently and
came out. The boy looked so much like a corpse
that many said, "He's dead." But Jesus took him
by the hand and lifted him to his feet, and he
stood up.

After Jesus had gone indoors, his disciples asked
him privately, "Why couldn't we drive it out?"

He replied, "This kind can come out only by
prayer."

The Five-step Prayer Model

The five-step model consists of the following:

1) The Interview – Here you question the person
to determine the condition for which prayer is
sought, and if possible, the cause of the condition.

The purpose here is to determine the root cause
of the infirmity or sickness. Possible root causes
can consist of an afflicting spirit; sickness rooted
in the soul (psychosomatic); or natural causes
such as accident, injury, or disease.

If the cause is known, then you can go immediately
to step 3) Prayer Selection. Typical questions are:
What is your name? How can I pray for you? How
long have you had this condition? Do you know
the cause? Did someone cause this condition?

You should be listening to them in the natural and
also listening for a word of knowledge. Depend
on the Holy Spirit—quietly ask Him if He has
anything to show you about the condition or its
cause. Listen to Him! You are listening, in both

cases, for what may be the root cause of the illness.

2) Prayer Selection – This is based upon the supposed root cause that you determined in the previous step. Obviously you would not pray the same way for someone who has an afflicting spirit as you would for someone who needed prayer for healing of past hurts. You would not pray for someone with a physical or bio-chemical disorder as you would for someone with an illness that is related to a spiritual root.

The two main categories of prayer are petition and command:

Petition: "Father, in Jesus' name I ask You to heal the inflammation in Joe's knee and take out the swelling and pain."

Command: "In the name of Jesus I command the inflammation in Joe's knee to be healed, and all swelling and pain to leave."

Commands are generally used when: breaking a curse or vow; casting out an afflicting spirit or other spirit; you have used petition prayers and progress has stopped; you are led to use them by the Holy Spirit; a word of knowledge; or other circumstances indicate that God wants to heal the person immediately (Many times a gift of faith manifests at this time and you know that a command will bring healing).

3) Prayer Ministry (Praying for Effect) – Prayer ministry should have an effect. Our goal is to see the person healed and the Name of Jesus Christ glorified. General steps to take consist of the following:

Audibly ask the Holy Spirit to be present with His guidance and His healing power.

Ask the person not to pray but instead, to close her eyes and focus on her body. It's a time to just receive.

Ask the person to interrupt you and tell you if/ when something is felt, i.e. heat/electricity/ trembling, etc. – about 50% of people being healed feel something.

If indicated, have the person confess any sin (unforgiveness, anger, etc.) and/or pray for the person's emotional healing before praying for physical healing.

Other helpful tips:

• Keep your eyes open to see God's touch.

• Follow any leading of the Holy Spirit.

• Use your normal tone of voice.

• Always pray in the name of Jesus.

• Use short, specific prayers.

• Pray where God is working.

• Periodically ask, "What is going on?" and "Are you feeling anything?"

- Remember- trust the Holy Spirit, not the method.

- Be loving! Be persistent!

- Thank God for whatever He does. You cannot thank God too much!

4) Stop and Re-interview — Keep listening to the Holy Spirit. Stop praying and re-interview the person.

Ask them how they are doing or what they are feeling while being prayed for. Depending upon the response of the individual, you may either want to continue praying the same way or in another manner. You want to continue praying for them the same way when they are feeling something happening to them. If nothing is happening then you may want to switch the way you are praying for that person. The object here is to find out what is happening so you can adjust your prayer to bless what the Father is doing.

If pain moves around or increases during prayer or if a condition has existed a long time, consider casting out an afflicting spirit.

Stop praying when: the person is healed or wants you to stop; the Holy Spirit tells you to stop; you are gaining no ground and receive no other way to pray.

5.) Post-prayer Suggestions – After praying, it is beneficial to give helpful, follow-up instructions or exhortations:

- Encourage the person from Scripture.

- Share appropriate lifestyle changes for maintaining healing and to prevent problem reoccurrence.

- Prepare the person to resist any further attack after healing.

- If someone is not healed or is only partially healed, do not accuse the person of a lack of faith or of sin in his or her life as the cause. Encourage them to keep coming for prayer and seeking God until the healing comes.

Ministry done *in love* is paramount. Many have continued to press in for healing who did not immediately receive because they were "so encouraged by the love of God that was present" whenthey were prayed for." The person prayed for should always leave with greater awareness of the Father and His love and care.

The difference in ministering healing in a crusade or renewal context and in a pastoral context has mainly been the time constraints. Even with a ministry team, there has been a different focus in the crusade or renewal meetings than that of a regular worship service on Sunday or a small group setting. Often there are hundreds of people needing to receive ministry during these times. Circumstances do not permit the amount of time I would normally spend while praying for someone for healing. In renewal meetings I usually do not pray for healing until later in the meetings. The only exception to this is if the ministry team and I receive words of knowledge for healing that night. Then I have a time for healing as part of the overall invitation.

I have already alluded to this, but I was deeply impacted in Toronto while reading the account of how Peter responded to the healing of the cripple at the Gate called Beautiful. He said "Why do you look at us as if by our own godliness or power this man has been healed?" Later he adds, "This man was healed by faith in the name of Jesus." I saw that Peter was what I called a Teflon Christian. He did not let any of the glory or honor stick to himself— he was always careful to give the glory and honor to Jesus. I also became much more concerned that the Name of Jesus was more prominent in my healing prayers than they had been before going to Toronto.

Catching

Why the need for catchers?

Like many others, I had heard the myth that states you don't need catchers because you will never get hurt when you fall under the Spirit's power. This myth says that if it is truly something God is doing, then you cannot possibly get hurt. In my experience, I found this not to be the truth. I discovered that some people had been hurt and experienced great pain when they fell. I also realized some found it difficult to receive from the Lord because they had a fear of falling and being hurt. Catchers made them able to relax and it was easier for them to receive from the Holy Spirit.

We must train catchers to catch in the meetings. It is one thing to have people catching — it is another to have them trained in how to catch people without hurting them. Many times when the people catching are not trained, they can catch the person falling in a way that is incorrect and they could end up injured.

I didn't think about training catchers until I saw a woman get hurt at my own church one of the first Sundays back from Toronto. I was praying for this woman during a time of ministry. Behind her was another woman who was prepared to catch her if she happened to fall to the floor. When she did fall, the woman behind her reached around and put both of her hands on the breasts of the woman who was falling as she was guiding her to the floor. Obviously this woman's experience was less pleasant because she didn't know if it was a man or a woman who had caught her. Sometimes men have had their shirts pulled up exposing much of their stomachs. At other times, women have been exposed as their blouses pulled up over their undergarments. These are significant reasons to train catchers, but they are not the only reasons.

Occasionally an untrained catcher would touch a person's back and then back away remove their hands, causing the person not to know whether anyone was still behind them. Even worse is when the person who receives prayer thinks that the catcher is still behind them and they fall with no support. Obviously, this can easily result in injury. On one such occasion someone fell and caught the corner of a metal chair, resulting in a gash in the head. Another elderly woman fell and hit her arm against a theatre-style chair. Her arm looked like it was definitely broken when she came to me. I prayed for her arm and encouraged her to go immediately to the emergency room to have it x-rayed. She refused to see a doctor even though I requested she should do so. When I called back to check up on her, however, I was told that God had healed her arm.

Another reason that I train catchers is because of the premium I place upon floor space. If the room is full of people seated and most of them want prayer, there is obviously not enough room if they were to all fall down under the power of God. It has not been uncommon for as many as 90% of the people to fall in some of the meetings. If there is no organization while praying for people, the floor space is not used efficiently. If someone in a line is allowed to fall sideways rather than straight back, then the next two to three people cannot be prayed for because if they were to fall, they would fall on the person who has fallen sideways.

We also found that training catchers is important for those who want to join the ministry team or expand their prayer ministry skills. For the catcher, there is an opportunity to learn how to cooperate with the Holy Spirit by hearing the prayer and watching the person respond to the Holy Spirit. Catching offers a low pressure environment to practice hearing from the Holy Spirit and watching how others who have been trained to cooperate with the Holy Spirit. The catcher will not actually pray out loud, but it is a good way for them to observe someone else operating in prayer ministry.

For these reasons I have training times for the catchers, as well as the rest of the ministry team.

Catching Tips

Following are basic instructions on how to catch:

- Make sure you are strong enough to catch those to whom you are assigned. If not, get help.

- Keep the tips of one hand touching the person's back so that they know you are there. STAY THERE! WE WANT NO SURPRISES!

- When catching, hold one hand above the other, so that as the person falls back, your hands do not unintentionally wrap around the person's torso, causing embarrassment to you both.

- Keep your feet apart, with one leg in front to help catch and continuously support the weight of the person as they slide down. This allows you to gently guide them to the floor, and allows you to cradle the person's head as you carefully set them down.

- Make sure that the person is in a comfortable position. Help them if requested or necessary.
  If a lot of activity is happening around them, such as others falling, remain and guard them from injury until things settle down (or get another to help, so that you can move on to further assist the one doing prayer ministry).

Summary

I hope what I have written will be of help to you. I caution you against turning my observations into laws rather than leaving them as observations. I consider them as principles, at best. I admit that God uses other people in a way that is very different from what I have talked about, and it really is God, so don't make my observations and suggestions "Saul's armor" for a young David. If God has blessed you in the use of the sling then use it. I was just sharing how I use my sling. My counsel to people when ministering to them works with the use of the sling God has given me. It could prove counterproductive if God has equipped you to minister in a different manner. So do not hear me saying that I have something better than you. What I have written is just the sharing of what works for me.

God bless you as you begin or continue the exciting ministry of cooperating with the Holy Spirit. Through Him we are enabled to become co-laborers with Christ.

Let the name of Jesus Christ be held in high honor in our cities as people witness healing and deliverances as we share the gospel of the Kingdom.

Healing Ministry in Your Church

Introduction

If you have been thinking of starting a healing ministry in your church, this booklet is for you.

If you already have a healing ministry, but it is not bringing results that stir your congregation, attract visitors, or interests the lost in the power of Jesus, this booklet might be for you.

If you have been wondering how to keep renewal alive in your church, this booklet may be for you.

The purpose of the booklet is to outline some of the things that pastors in the United States who have vibrant healing ministries in their churches have proved essential or helpful. It is intended to help you transform what may be a vision into reality.

The Key Person

The key person in your church, if you want to have an active, successful healing ministry, is *you.*

Pastors who have successful healing ministries say that they regard their **support** and **participation** as essential to the healing ministry in their churches. If you are not enthusiastic about having a healing ministry in your church, you will probably not do the things necessary to start or keep such a ministry alive. Your congregation sensing this, will take its cue from you.

Even if you have some people who *are* excited about praying for the sick, they will gradually lose their strong sense of purpose if you are not enthusiastically involved as the senior pastor. Their ministry will gradually become just another one of the worth-while activities in your church, contributing to its life to some degree, but not generating excitement in your congregation or serving as a stimulus for outreach into your community.

How can you get excited about a healing ministry?

The best way to get excited about having a healing ministry is to see a strong healing ministry in action, where miracles of healing are *expected,* and where they occur on a *regular* basis.

The best way I know to see such a ministry in action is to go on an international trip with Global Awakening or another organization that uses ministry teams extensively, where you and other leaders like yourself join with many believers (God's "little ol' mes") to pray for the sick in meeting after meeting. On such a trip, seeing miracle after miracle of healing, you will almost certainly become interested in having a vital healing ministry in your church– it has happened to literally dozens of pastors!

You can experience the same sort of thing on a reduced scale at our meetings in the United States. Our yearly Voice of the Apostles conferences and the Healing Schools which we present at various cities in North America have been the catalyst for many pastors to begin having powerful healing ministries in their churches.

If the prospect of participating in such a ministry with Global Awakening interests you, visit our website at www. globalawakening.com, where you can get our schedule for contacting us for information about each trip or meeting.

Another option is for you to visit a church that has a vital healing ministry. One such church is Bethel Church in Redding, California, pastored by Bill Johnson.[1] Bill has traveled extensively with me and his church has such a reputation that people come to them from a wide area to receive prayer for healing. You may know of such a church in your neighborhood.

How can your church become enthusiastic about a healing ministry?

Perhaps the most effective way of getting church members enthusiastic about praying for healings is for them to attend an evangelistic crusade where believers of all ages and from all walks of live do much of the praying for the sick. When they see ordinary people like themselves pray for sick people and see healings take place before their eyes, or when they themselves pray for sick people and see many of them get healed, they are likely to become enthusiastic about participating in a healing ministry.

As pastor, you might consider inviting several of your congregation to accompany you on an outreach where much prayer for the sick occurs.

However, even if attending a ministry trip or another church's healing ministry is not practicable for you, you can still start or improve a healing ministry in your church by initiating training for your interested people and then encouraging them to step out with you in praying for the sick. Training with actual hands-on practice is very helpful. The most important thing, though, is your own participation and encouragement.

[1] *You can contact Bill Johnson at info@bethel.org*

Why Have a Healing Ministry in Your Church?

A strong healing ministry in your church will help you stay true to the gospel: a gospel of the Kingdom and a gospel of power.

A strong healing ministry in your church is effective in evangelizing the lost and as an aid to church growth.

C. Peter Wagner, a former professor of church growth at Fuller Theological seminary, points out that by far the fastest church growth worldwide is in those countries where there is widespread healing activity in the church and that, although there are exceptions, the churches in those countries that have active healing ministries tend to be those showing the greatest growth.[2]

Ramsay McMullen, a historian at Yale University who studied the spread of Christianity into the Roman Empire, comments that the "Christianization" of the empire was due primarily to the impact of Christians healing the sick and casting out demons.[3] I think of Paul, who described his coming to the church in Corinth—after preaching with little effect in Athens—thus:

[3] *C. Peter Wagner, How to Have a Healing Ministry in Any Church, 1988, Regal, a division of Gospel Light, Ventura, CA, chap. 3.*
[4] *Ramsay MacMullen, Christianizing the Roman Empire, AD 100-400, 1984, Yale University Press, New Haven, CT, p. 27; cited in Wagner, op cit., p. 76.*

And I, brethren, when I came to you, did not come with excellence of speech or of wisdom declaring to you the testimony of God. For I determined not to know anything among you except Jesus Christ and Him crucified. I was with you in weakness, in fear, and in much trembling. And my speech and my preaching were not with persuasive words of human wisdom, but in demonstration of the Spirit and of power, that your faith should not be in the wisdom of men but in the power of God. 1 Cor. 2:1-5 (NKJV).

I have talked with pastors in China whose underground churches have grown enormously in recent years. They told me that eighty to ninety percent of their new believers have come to the Lord because they were healed through prayer or knew of someone who was so healed.

A Word About Renewal

Many churches have experienced something often called "renewal" or "revival," generally involving meetings at which the Holy Spirit touches people deeply—sometimes without manifestations, but frequently with the manifestations of trembling, falling, resting trance-like, weeping, laughing, and others. Those who are touched in this way (and many not touched in this way, but present in these same meetings) often have a strong sense of God's presence, gain a renewed interest in a God-centered life, experience healing of emotional wounds, and frequently find new empowerment for a ministry that was in danger of ending due to burnout.

Churches hope to see such meetings continue indefinitely and regard these manifestations as evidence that all is well with the church and its members. However, far too often these marvelous and powerful sessions fade into rather ordinary meetings with sometimes wonderful praise and worship, but with considerably reduced effect on individual lives and little lasting effect on the church. In my view, this often happens because the emphasis in the church is on continued visitations of the Holy Spirit with these manifestations (something of an unconscious, well-meaning "bless me" attitude), without the adequate outward expression of a "servant heart"—moving out to do what the Holy Spirit (as shown perhaps in large part through these manifestations) has been equipping the members of the church to do.

Generally speaking, I believe the Holy Spirit is interested in equipping the saints for the work of ministry, including evangelism, missions, visiting those in prison, helping the poor, ministering to the sick and those in bondage, other works of charity, and activities intended to bring the power and love of God into secular activities. If the church does not move on into servant-ministry, it may languish in seeking continued outward manifestations of the Holy Spirit's presence.

Praying for the sick is one of the ministries a church can engage in that will help keep the power of the Holy Spirit flowing. It's an easy ministry to engage in, because every interested member can participate, and because it does not require a substantial investment of funds. It ought not to be the only ministry the church engages in, but it is one of the things that can help a church to remain in renewal. It can also be a stepping stone to evangelism and to other outreaches of various kinds that please God and keep the river of the Spirit flowing.

"Praying for the sick was an obvious and necessary outflow of revival. We did not believe we could continue in revival without following the Lord's example in pursuing this essential aspect of ministry." – Bill Johnson

The Place of the Pastor

As expressed in the introduction, a prerequisite to a successful healing ministry is the desire and commitment of the senior pastor of the church. By his words and his actions he must communicate that he considers such a ministry of great importance to his church. If he does, many in his congregation will also consider it of great importance. If the senior pastor places a healing ministry lower on his list of priorities, his congregation will sense his attitude and will also consider it of less importance.

This may not mean a big investment of time, but it does mean an investment of quality time and quality thought. You may not be the actual leader of the ministry; it can be an associate or a layman. But the ministry will require your participation, and both the leader and the ministry must have your unequivocal, enthusiastic support.

As the pastor or senior pastor, you must be willing to lead by example. Successful pastors suggest the following ways you can lead:

- *Personally going on evangelistic crusades where many layman participate in praying for the sick.*

- *Becoming familiar with training and resource materials.*

- *Receiving training yourself of the kind and model that your ministry team is receiving.*

- *Inviting people to receive prayer during or after every regular service, with prayer usually by a "team" that includes laymen.*

- *Expanding the other occasions in your church where people are invited to receive prayer, not necessarily by "team" members, but by those in attendance at the occasion.*

- *Frequently joining the ministry team when it is praying for the sick, even if you do not consider yourself particularly anointed for healing. You'll grow, and they will be encouraged to press in by your example.*

- *Getting prayer when you are sick or in pain, and testifying if you are healed through the prayer.*

- *Especially important is to vigorously encourage testimonies of healing at every opportunity.*

As pastor, you will need to give open, strong, and consistent support for things that strengthen the healing ministry in your church. This includes training, regular ministry times; support of the ministry team and its leadership; constant encouragement of testimonies; inviting visiting speakers with strong healing ministries; recognition of those who serve; and seeking impartation for yourself and your church members from those who may have greater anointing for healing.

"It is essential...that the senior pastor be involved. The senior pastor is the one who sets the standard and people aren't going to grow too far past his mark."
–Bill Johnson

"It is essential that I stay involved...that I model praying for the sick. The team needs to see me experience the same successes and failures that they have."
–Tom Jones[4]

The Place of Preaching

Pastors with successful healing ministries in their churches preach seriously on healing from time to time. Common topics preached include:

- *Healing the sick is a significant spiritual ministry.*

- *Healing was a central part of Jesus' ministry.*

- *The mission and charge to the disciples set out in Luke 9 and 10 specifically included healing the sick.*

- *Jesus used healing to demonstrate that He was the Messiah (Luke 4:18-21; 5:20-26; 7:18-23).*

- *Jesus regarded sickness and demonic oppression as works of the devil. Luke 13:16; 11:20.*

- *Healing is in the Atonement. Isaiah 53:5.*

- *The frequent connection between healing and evangelism in the Book of Acts.*

[4] *Tom Jones is former Senior Pastor of Suncoast Worship Center and currently serves as the Executive Director of A.N.G.A*

- *The importance of healing in evangelism today. God's heart is to heal. Jesus is a revelation of God's heart. Mark 1:41.*

- *The importance of persistence in praying for the sick.*

- *The Great Commission. "Therefore go and make disciples of all nations, baptizing them in the name of the Father and of the Son and of the Holy Spirit, 20 and teaching them to obey everything I have commanded you. And surely I am with you always, to the very end of the age" (Matt. 28:19-20; Mark 16:15-18).*

- *"Thy kingdom come on earth as it is in heaven." (There is no sickness in heaven) Matt. 6:10.*

See also "A Biblical Basis for Healing" and "Ministry Team Training Manual" by Randy Clark.

The Place of a "Ministry Team"

If a church is to develop an effective healing ministry, the "little ol' mes" of the church—not *just* the pastor and not *just* the pastor and elders or deacons—**must** be involved in the ministry. Usually this will start in the form of lay men and women who have had training and who, sometimes along side you, pray for the sick on a regular basis in church services, under the direction and with the approval of the church leadership.

If lay people are not involved, there is little chance that the ministry will extend outside the church building itself. Even with lay people involved, extension of the ministry beyond the walls of the church building will usually require your active encouragement.

To allow for more people to serve on your ministry team, in the event of absences, and to avoid burn-out of team members, you may want enough team members so that they can rotate assignments. As a pastor, I used two separate teams, each with its own leader, for our two Sunday services.

You may want enough team members so that each team member needs to serve only every second or third Sunday.

Where, When, and by Whom?

Praying for the sick can be part of the regular Sunday church service, or it can take place after the Sunday church service, or it can take place at a special meeting, such as every Sunday night, the first Friday night of each month, etc, at all gatherings of church members, or any or all of the above.

It is important that praying for the sick take place on a regular basis, so that it becomes an integral part of the life of the church.

"Healing is not something you add to the church; it should be a part of the fiber of your church. It should be a part of every ministry. It's not a finger or arm attached to the body; it's more like the blood which flows throughout the body" –Tom Jones

At Bethel Church, there is prayer for the sick at every meeting of the congregation, "...on Friday, Saturday, and Sunday and throughout the week." Bill Johnson says, "No time is better than another, but when the Holy Spirit is prompting, always be ready."

Praying for the sick should not end with the ministry team. From the ministry team it should expand to most of the members of the church. Some of this ministry will be by groups of two or more individuals while some of it will be by one person ministering alone.

At Bethel Church, everyone– whether the senior pastor, an associate pastor, a staff person, a secretary, a janitor– is trained and ready to pray for the sick as they come into the church.

"If you are a teacher, pray for the sick. If you are an usher, pray for the sick. If you are a greeter, pray for the sick. I teach that no matter where your area of giftedness lies, you can still heal the sick." –Tom Jones

Thirdly, prayer for the sick should not end in the church.

Taking Healing Outside the Church and to the Streets

From the church it should expand to many places outside the church. Much of the evangelistic power of healing will be realized outside the church building.

At the outset, I'm sure a new ministry team will be most comfortable praying for the sick in a familiar setting, such as in a church service or home group. However, some of your congregation, especially if you encourage them, will find opportunities outside of these settings. There are many occasions outside of church that offer perhaps brief but very effective opportunities for prayer. Here are some examples:

- *A telephone conversation with someone who has fear about something, or a "splitting headache," or a sprain or strain, or an ache or pain of some kind.*

- *The visitor in a home who has an illness or injury.*

The workman or service man who comes to a home or office, and who has an illness or injury.

- *The waitress in a restaurant.*
- *The flight attendant on an airplane.*

- *A colleague in a business meeting.*

- *A business customer.*

Some individuals and groups of young people at Bethel Church walk through a mall or any other public place, offering to pray for anyone who seems to need prayer. Bill Johnson comments "If you are going to embrace the ministry of healing, you have to be ready and willing to do it anytime, anywhere." And, "Our highest percent of success is out on the streets in the public places."

Some churches send out teams of two or three to call "cold" on homes, identifying themselves as Christians or as members of a church, and asking if anyone in the home is sick and would like prayer for healing. Frequently there is someone who would like prayer, and often healing follows, with a resulting evangelistic opportunity.

Some churches send out a team of two or three women to pray for a sick woman in her home, or a team of two or three men to pray for a sick man in his home. Frequently healings result, with wonderful testimonies.

Many ministries to the poor, as in the distribution of food and clothing, afford opportunities for praying for sick people who are visited or who come for food.

At Suncoast Worship Center, some teams leave as early as 4:30 am for places where day laborers are working, to give the men and women a sack lunch and then pray for all who will allow them.

Testimonies of such activities outside the "four walls" itself are very inspiring, in my view, even if initial results are not at first great. God blesses these activities, often with greater results than come from prayers for believers in the building, indicating how highly He values them. Such testimonies can be very powerful.

The Place of Excitement (or, How to Get Started)

Divine healing is always supernatural. It is always miraculous. Sometimes it is spectacular, as when a very serious condition or a condition of long duration, is suddenly healed through prayer. Even a "minor miracle," such as the lengthening of a short arm or leg, the sudden end to a headache, or relief from pain in a throbbing thumb, can be astonishing to someone who has never seen a miracle.

As I noted in the introduction, probably the best way to get your church started or to have your ministry team's spirits raised, is for several members of the church to participate in a crusade where "little ol' mes" do much of the praying, and where many healings occur. Their resulting enthusiasm and mutual support are often the spark that ignites an effective healing ministry.

> *"Take some of your ministry team on a ministry trip where they can have intense exposure over a short period of time. On a ministry trip they will pray for more people and see more happen in a week or two than they will probably see in several months in their church."*
> –Tom Jones

Or, I might add, perhaps in several years in their church.

When healings occur on a regular basis, more church members will want to get involved in the ministry. Members will bring sick relatives and friends for prayer, and these in turn will speak about the healing services to their friends and families. An effective healing ministry can bring vitality to a sleepy church and more enthusiasm to a live one.

The Place of Testimonies

Constant encouragement of testimonies of healing by the senior pastor is essential.

Nothing arouses interest and excitement more than seeing a person healed. The next best thing is to hear the person who was healed tell about her condition and her healing. For this reason it is exceedingly important to encourage those who have been healed through prayer to tell the church what has happened.

Testimonies are important for building faith in the congregation and for attracting to Jesus those visitors in the congregation who don't know Him. In my view, the importance of testimonies cannot be overstated; Testimonies should be given to all the church, so that all know what is happening.

Where testimonies have not been the practice, there may be reluctance on the part of those healed to speak up, and there may be reluctance on your part as the pastor to encourage speaking up. However, the encouragement of your people to testify to their healings is essential.

As the senior pastor you should mention the imortance of testimonies for building faith and for evangelism to the whole church, especially first, and periodically thereafter. You should tell your church that, on every suitable occasion, you intend to include testimonies:

- *By persons healed through prayer in the church.*

- *By persons healed through prayer in home groups.*

- *By persons who prayed for someone outside the "four walls" at the office, at the check-out counter, on the street, on the telephone, at the soup kitchen, at the restaurant, or over coffee at home.*

I would like to stress again that in my view, just the fact that a church member prayed for someone outside the church service or small group is important and worth sharing. If healing also occurred, that is a great plus. Testimonies of healings that occur outside the church building are especially valuable.

Then, you should follow through by actually requesting testimonies, not as an afterthought nor as an incidental activity, but as an important part of the service. Don't worry if sometimes no one responds to testify.

The extent to which you encourage testimonies will do more than anything else to show the value you and your church place on the healing ministry (or, for that matter, on any other activity). Another indication is your encouragement for every member of your church to become a "minister." Praying for the sick and ministry to the poor are perhaps the two easiest ways for a believer to become involved in ministry outside the church building.

A number of years ago, I visited a large church in Kiev, Ukraine, pastored by Henry Madava. At each of the several meetings I attended, after welcoming guests, Henry asked the congregation to respond to some questions by raising their hands: "Did you share the gospel with someone this week? Did you lead someone to Christ this week? Is a person you led to the Lord this week here with you now?" Then he invited some of the pairs—the church member and the new believer—to tell the church what happened.

After this, Henry asked the congregation, "Did you pray for someone to be healed this week outside of the church services? Did the person you prayed for get healed?" Then a couple of those who responded affirmatively were invited to testify about the healing.

This practice clearly showed the church that evangelism and healings, with all members "doing the stuff," were high values for him and for the church.

At Bethel Church folks who are healed often testify at once, immediately after receiving a healing. If the healing occurs in church, the person testifies to the church. If in a staff or board meeting, the person testifies to the staff or the board, and may later testify to the church. Pastor Bill Johnson explains "We look hard for testimonies and give them in every meeting, including staff and board meetings."

I believe a testimony should be of an actual healing. If a person is only somewhat better, it may be best to wait until he is completely healed before having him testify. I think it is wise to avoid a testimony by someone who has not been healed, but who is "believing for my healing."

The Centrality of Training

There are different models for praying for the sick. A good one is set out in our "Ministry Team Training Manual". It is easy to learn and easy to practice. It is a help, if your ministry team has never had training, to ask a Global Awakening associate or some other competent teacher to hold training sessions for yourself and for the members and prospective members of your ministry team.I simply ask the pastors and lay people who accompany me to get training in the use of the model presented in the Manual.

The training you choose should include the importance of character, of love, and of compassion. It should include such practical items as praying with eyes open, using one's normal tone of voice, laying on of hands, and the use of catchers. It should include the importance of persistence, the importance of discovering and dealing with causes of an illness or other condition, recognition of hindrances to healing, and the effectiveness of short prayers with frequent checks for progress when praying for conditions where improvement is easy to recognize.

It is important that a ministry team member have absolute confidence that God loves the person being prayed for, and that God's love, through him or her, will bless the person even if physical healing does not occur. Teaching on this aspect of ministry is important.

I believe prayer for healing should be made with the expectation that God will answer the prayer at the time it is prayed—that is, that healing or at least improvement will follow immediately. Those who pray should pray with *expectancy*! Actual practice in praying for sick people and seeing healings is a very good confidence builder.

However, a team member should also be prepared to spend time perhaps considerable time—with the seeker. In some cases, "soaking prayer" is needed. Prayers of 20 or 30 minutes are not unusual in our meetings. At times, one or more team members may spend the whole worship time, or perhaps the entire ministry time, praying quietly for one person. Team members should appreciate that sometimes ministry may involve inconvenience, discomfort, and perhaps sacrifice.

Of course, healing does not always follow the prayer time. The team member must be prepared for this. Here again, teaching or training is important.

Other elements of significance might be following an established "gender policy" in the church, the use of oil when praying for the sick, whether prayers minister alone or with partners, and observance of other church's policies.

A good summary of helpful training is included in the Global Awakening training manual, mentioned above, in the sections on prayer guidelines and team protocol, and in the several sections on healing.

Tom Jones, for example, used his own manual. He also used experienced visiting teachers, but did most of the training himself. When you are ready, it would be a positive step if you undertake to do part of the training of your team yourself.

Who Should Receive Training?

Probably every member of your church who prays for the sick should receive training. Rigidity and legalism are not necessary, but general uniformity encourages confidence in the congregation and helps to avoid weird or other unhelpful mannerisms.

Since it is good for everyone on staff or serving in any capacity to be able to pray for the sick, each of them should receive training. If the pastoral staff follows a different model from the one taught to the ministry team, confusion will be introduced.

In both Bethel Church and Suncoast Worship Center, all leaders are involved on the ministry team, and all follow the same general model.

Both pastors consider their participation and that of other church leaders on the ministry team as essential, and they all receive the same training as the ministry team. Both of them encourage all members of the congregation to receive training and to pray for the sick whenever the occasion presents itself.

Common Pastoral Hesitations

There are several places where you may be tempted to omit essential or valuable elements of a successful healing ministry. Here are some, with a few comments about them:

1) You may be tempted to skip the training for yourself or other leaders in the church, or perhaps for all who have had considerable experience in praying for the sick. You may think the training is not needed, or perhaps that it is beneath the dignity of the church leaders.

Answer: *This is a mistake. Appropriate training will increase the effectiveness of most pray-ers, even leaders. Many experienced pray-ers do not really expect healing to follow quickly when they pray. Training will build confidence if it includes practice by the attendees in praying for people with actual needs. And will also help to avoid weird or odd methods of praying will avoid the confusion that can result if different prayer models are used by various members of the ministry team and it will help you to identify with your ministry team.*

2) You may be tempted not to encourage testimonies. You may think testimonies take too long.

Answer: *Some testimonies may indeed be too long. Short testimonies may especially be needed where there are several or many who wish to testify. Experience will help to determine when to avoid too-lengthy testimonies. Some suggestions:*

- *Let the interviewer hold the microphone, not the one giving the testimony.*

- *Let the interviewer encourage the person to be brief: "Please tell us what was wrong in just five words."*

- *He can ask limiting questions, such as "Did you feel anything – heat, electricity or did the pain just go?"*

However, I would encourage you not to shut down testimonies much. You are much more likely than the members of your congregation to think a testimony is too long. Your congregation may find a testimony much more interesting than you do.

3) You may think testimonies take time from more important things such, as your preaching the Word.

Answer: *The Word is indeed of great importance. However, actual evidence of the love and the power of God is also of great importance! Let's face it. It's possible that a testimony showing the power of God to heal may speak more to your congregation, and thus do more for the Kingdom, than the same amount of time added to a particular sermon! Note what Paul wrote in 1 Corinthians 2:1-5:*

¹When I came to you, brothers, I did not come with eloquence or superior wisdom as I proclaimed to you the testimony about God. ²For I resolved to know nothing while I was with you except Jesus Christ and him crucified. ³I came to you in weakness and fear, and with much trembling. ⁴My message and my preaching were not with wise and persuasive words, but with a demonstration of the Spirit's power, ⁵so that your faith might not rest on men's wisdom, but on God's power.

A testimony can be an illuminating teaching tool. It can sometimes be used as a spring-board for comments about the love of God, the power of God, the boldness of the pray-er, the manner of praying, the working of the Holy Spirit, etc. Can we see a healing testimony as an aid to our preaching, rather than as a competitor with our preaching?

4) You may hesitate to pray for the sick yourself, worrying that some members of the congregation will get more healings when they pray for the sick than you do, and that you may accordingly lose status.

Answer: *I have to face the fact that some laymen are more anointed for healing than I am. We pastors need to develop a Kingdom view about this—God's Kingdom, not ours! We may need to repent of insecurity, perhaps jealousy, perhaps fear, and learn to sincerely rejoice when a "little ol' me" is more anointed than we are for healing or, for that matter, in any other spiritual gifting.*

5) You may feel that encouraging testimonies also encourages spiritual pride.

Answer: *Spiritual pride can indeed develop when a ministry team or a team member has many successes in praying for the sick. Cautions may be needed, but don't let that concern override the greater good that sharing testimonies brings in releasing kingdom realities through the power of the testimony and bringing glory to God.*

6) You may be tempted to stop asking for testimonies if some meetings go by without anyone reporting a healing.

Answer: *Persistence in requesting testimonies is vital! Encourage them to share, even about healings that seem "minor."*

7) You may be tempted to stop having prayer for the sick if not many people report being healed or if some who receive prayer remain ill or die.

Answer: *Persistence in praying for the sick is vital! Tom Jones says, "Never, never, never give up or quit. The Holy Spirit told me years ago, after I prayed diligently for a 24-year-old who died of cancer, 'You pray for the sick and leave the rest to Me.'"*

A note to items 5 and 6: Preaching on persistence is very useful. There are many examples of successful healing ministries that started out very poorly as far as results were concerned: John Wimber, Heidi Baker, Charles and Frances Hunter, and my own ministry, are some examples.

8) You may be tempted to cancel the prayers for the sick on occasions when interesting events occur.

Answer: *Praying for the sick should be consistent. It should be an integral part of each service.*

The Place of Words of Knowledge for Healing

Words of knowledge for healing are really words from God that He is prepared to heal persons with a particular disease or condition now—at this time!

Words of knowledge for healing are particularly faith-building. You will probably see a higher percentage of healings when words of knowledge for healing are given than in the usual prayer times. You should by all means be prepared to encourage words of knowledge from members of your congregation, including the member who takes his courage in hand and steps out, but feels his "word" was not accurate.

When a condition that has been called out publicly is healed, it is a clear demonstration to unbelievers in the midst of the love of God and His power to heal, and can be a very good opportunity for evangelism.

Tom Jones encouraged members of his church to give words of knowledge at any point in his services.

If words of knowledge for healing are new to you and your ministry team, consider having someone visit who is skilled in encouraging people to try them. This may give you and your ministry team a jump-start in using them.

I frequently teach on how to receive and use words of knowledge for healing, and usually there are many in the audience who have never given a word of knowledge in public.

I usually ask for words of knowledge, but only from those who have never given one publicly. I don't think I have ever had a group that did not begin actually having many accurate words of knowledge.

The Place of Encouragement

Unfailing encouragement should be your rule as the pastor.

The various needs for encouragement have been mentioned above. It is perhaps enough to say here that if there is not strong encouragement from the senior pastor, the experience of the ministry team will drop a bit then from there the expectations of those who minister will drop a bit, and then their experience will drop again, and then their expectancy will drop again, etc, resulting in a downward spiral. Strong encouragement from you as the pastor can prevent this.

As noted earlier, occasional exposure to meetings where a vital healing ministry is taking place is also extremely helpful and important in this respect.

The Place of Intercession

Intercession is very important here, as in all aspects of the life of your church. If there is no intercessory prayer group in your church, pray for the Lord to raise one up and to guide you in it.

The intercessors as individuals should be trained in praying for the sick, but it is not necessary that they join the ministry team. It *is* important for them to pray for the effectiveness and success of the healing ministry in the church, along with their other intercessory activities. We have found in our travels with teams around the world that those who also participate in the healing prayer ministry many times are also much more effective in their intercession times as a result of the experience.

At Bethel Church there is an intercessory group whose sole mission is to pray for the healing anointing in the church.

The Place of Impartation

Scripture is clear that there can be an impartation of spiritual gifting through prayer and the laying on of hands (Timothy 4:14). It is most desirable for you as pastor, and for members of the ministry team or perhaps even others, to receive prayer for impartation whenever practicable. There may be special opportunities for such impartation at crusades, or when a healing evangelist visits your church, for example, Bill Johnson encourages everyone to receive prayer for impartation whenever anyone who seems to have a strong anointing for healing is available.

At our crusades, I frequently devote an entire meeting to the subject of impartation, after which I pray for impartation for those specially moved upon by the Holy Spirit. I encourage team members—whether pastors or laymen— who feel so moved, to remove their ministry badges and receive impartation along with others from the crowd who come forward for this ministry.

The Place of the Visiting Teacher or Evangelist

If a visiting evangelist or speaker has an effective healing ministry, by all means take advantage of his presence for teaching, for ministering to your congregation if he is willing and for praying for you and others for impartation. Let the teaching be for all the congregation, if appropriate, and impartation for all who are moved by the Holy Spirit, whether or not they are on the ministry team. Rejoice when more people in the pews are called into a healing ministry.

Selection of Ministry Team Members

Age is not usually a valid criterion for team members. Qualified children, teenagers, adults, and seniors can serve effectively. In some churches there are "children's church", where the entire ministry team is made up of children.

Spiritual maturity may be a valid criterion. Team members should be reasonably stable, able to keep confidences, and making reasonable progress in their own spiritual lives. If there are spiritual or mental problems that might compromise the integrity of the ministry, help should be provided to assist the person in resolving the problems before releasing them to join the ministry team.

Important Elements in Healing Ministry

I have asked Bill and Tom to mention a few of what they see as very important elements for the development of the healing ministries in their churches.

Comments from Bill Johnson:

- We don't stop. No matter who dies, no matter who doesn't get healed, we just don't stop.

- We stay connected with people who have greater success than we do.

- We make room for prayer for the sick at every single meeting. We always make room for God to show up and touch people. It's either at the beginning, middle, or end of the meeting, or all of the above.

- "(Start) it. Be hungry and desperate enough for it that you are willing to receive from others who are successful already. Let them minister to you, learn to receive impartation from everyone who has a healing anointing, whether he is a great leader who travels the world or a fairly new believer who has great success in ministry. Let them pray for you."

• "No matter what, don't stop! It is impossible for you to pursue this ministry and not have success."

Comments from Tom Jones:

• We placed a high value on exposure to visiting leaders with strong healing and teaching ministries.

• We had ongoing training for the ministry team, and encouraged the entire congregation to become involved in praying for the sick.

• We set aside specific times to pray for the sick. Although we pray for the sick in every service, Sunday night was specifically devoted to this ministry. It's easier to have extended times of prayer at those special meetings. The folks prayed as long as they liked. We started at 6:00 and stopped when everyone left. There was no specific quitting time.

Some Additional Thoughts

I hope the following will be helpful to you in starting a healing ministry in your church or in helping one to thrive. Here are some other ideas that some churches are using that you might find interesting:

• Some churches train young people, and even children, to pray for the sick and encourage them to serve on the church's ministry team.
• Henry Madava, referred to earlier, pastors in the Ukraine where the fields are practically virgin

because of the atheism forced on the country by the former Soviet Union for decades; He sends teams of pray-ers out two by two ahead of himself into towns where he plans to have an evangelistic crusade. They visit hospitals, call on government offices, walk the streets, pray for anyone they can who is sick, and invite people to Henry's upcoming meetings. He reports extraordinary results.

Would this be possible in areas of our large cities?

• The pastor of a small church on the west coast visits the Philippines with a ministry team for two weeks or so every spring. Part of the time the ministry team separates the members going to different churches or institutions at the request of the local churches to pray for the sick, or for other special purposes with praying for the sick following. The rest of the time this pastor conducts public evening meetings, with prayer for the sick following each meeting. Daytimes, teams follow up those who have made decisions the night before and also offer to pray for any needs in the homes they call on. His ministry team gets a lot of practice praying for the sick in a very short time. Many healings result with great impact on any new team members.

Would joining such a mission in a third-world country be a possibility for you? Would organizing and leading such a mission be a possibility for you?

- "Occasionally, as I felt led, I would place 4 or 5 chairs down front and tell the people that anyone can come forward at any point during the praise and worship to sit in one of the chairs, and a team would "soak" him or her in prayer. This has worked extremely well." –Tom Jones

Conclusion

I'd like to close with a testimony. An event in a mid-western church illustrates a number of things spoken of above: that God uses children effectively for healing, that ministry outside the church building itself is especially powerful, and the effect of testimony.

> A boy of twelve saw a woman on the street, limping. In child-like confidence, he approached and asked if he could pray for her. She assented. It turns out that she had a bad knee and, when the boy prayed for her knee, it was healed! This of course impressed the lady tremendously, increased his faith level, and had quite an impact on the congregation when he recounted what the Lord had done!

I encourage you to catch a vision for healing ministry in YOUR church. Our Father loves to pour out His gifts upon His children! It is His will for us to receive answers to prayer, thereby extending His Kingdom and glorifying the Name of our Lord Jesus Christ. I pray that this booklet is effective in helping you to get a healing ministry started in your church.

Resource Materials

Many books have been written on the subject of praying for the sick. Some are considered classics, such as:

The Real Faith, Charles S. Price.

Christ the Healer, F. F. Bosworth.

God's Generals, Roberts Liardon.

God's Medicine Bottle (Pamphlet), Derek Prince.

Healing, Francis MacNutt.

How to Have a Healing Ministry in Any Church, C. Peter Wagner.

How to Heal the Sick, Charles and Frances Hunter.

John G. Lake, His Life, His Sermons, His Boldness of Faith, A compilation by Kenneth Copeland.

Power Evangelism, John Wimber, with Kevin Springer.

When Heaven Invades Earth, Bill Johnson.

Other books by Randy Clark

Entertaining Angels

There Is More

Power, Holiness and Evangelism

Lighting Fires

Changed in a Moment

Training Manuals Available

Ministry Team Training Manual

Schools of Healing and Impartation Workbooks

Core Message Series

Words of Knowledge

Biblical Basis of Healing

Baptism in the Holy Spirit

Open Heaven

Pressing In

The Thrill of Victory / The Agony of Defeat

Awed by Grace

n "There Is More," Randy lays a solid biblical foundation for a the-
ology of impartation, and takes a historical look at impartation and
visitation of the Lord in the Church. This is combined with personal
testimonies of people who have received an impartation throughout
the world and what the impact has been in their lives. You are taken
on journey throughout the world to see for yourself the lasting fruit that
is taking place in the harvest field - particularly in Mozambique. This
release of power is not only about phenomena of the Holy Spirit, it is
about its ultimate effect on evangelism and missions. Your heart will
be stirred for more as you read this book.

This is the book that Randy Clark was born to write."

- Bill Johnson

Vision

To release followers of Christ into their specific destiny and calling, in order to live out the Great Commission.

Structure

Global School of Supernatural Ministry is a one or two year ministry school with an emphasis on impartation and equipping students for a life of walking in the supernatural. Classes start each September and end the following May. Courses are offered on-site at the Apostolic Resource Center in Mechanicsburg, PA. Upon completion of each program year a Certificate of Completion is awarded. Students seeking additional educational training may do so while attending GSSM through the Wagner Leadership Institute.

Community

The GSSM student body is diverse in age, culture, ministry experience, and educational accomplishments. From high school graduates to professionals to retirees - the students come together seeking more of God. Supernatural power, passion and honor are key values of GSSM and are reflected in our worship, outreach and personal relationships.

For more information - or to enroll in classes - contact us at
1-866-AWAKENING or apply online at
http://gssm.globalawakening.com

globalawakening

For a schedule of upcoming events and conferences, or to purchase other products from Global Awakening, please visit our website at:

http://www.globalawakening.com